War Time

War Time Experiences recounts the memories and experiences of Donald Arthur Marlow during the Second World War. Born on the 9th of May, 1917, he continues to reside in Northamptonshire, and is a proud father, grandfather, and great grandfather. At the time of publishing (2012), Donald has celebrated his 95th birthday.

Copyright © 2012 by Donald Arthur Marlow

All rights reserved.

No part of this book may be reproduced in any form or by any electronic or mechanical means including information storage and retrieval systems, without permission in writing from the author. The only exception is by a reviewer, who may quote short excerpts in a review.

Although the author and publisher have made every effort to ensure that the information in this book was correct at press time, the author and publisher do not assume and hereby disclaim any liability to any party for any loss, damage, or disruption caused by errors or omissions, whether such errors or omissions result from negligence, accident, or any other cause.

Donald Arthur Marlow

Printed in the United Kingdom

First Printing: December 2012

ISBN 978-1-291-21672-1

DONALD ARTHUR MARLOW

WAR TIME EXPERIENCES

1939 – 1946

INTRODUCTION

I have been prevailed upon by members of my family to set down my wartime experiences from 1939 to 1946.

CHAPTER ONE – SEPTEMBER 1939

I first of all remember listening with Mary to the radio news at 11.00am, Sunday 3rd of September 1939, that we were now at war with Germany. Having been married at 1.15pm, on the 24th of December 1938, at St Peters Church Leicester, by the Curate the Rev. Rumsey (incidentally, we were the first couple to be married by him), our wedding reception was enjoyed by relatives and friends at 'The Barrel' public house in Leicester. We could not afford a Honeymoon, so after the reception we caught a train from Leicester main railway station to Desborough, Northamptonshire, six inches deep in snow, and we walked to our new house, 'Fieldsview', Dunkirk Avenue, Desborough, which we purchased from my father Arthur Marlow by virtue of the fact that he gave us the deposit, and a loan was arranged with Desborough Co-operative Society. My mother and father provided all the furniture, carpets etc., so we had a good start; needless to say, we were very happy. Mary loved that house and she was singing and polishing all day.

As I knew at the age of 22 I would be liable to be 'called up', I wrote to the War Office in October 1939 enquiring if they had any vacancies in the Royal Engineers, and also how one could obtain a commission. I received a reply that there were no vacancies in the Royal Engineers, and all commissions would be obtained after serving through the ranks. This was a complete falsehood because when I eventually became a sapper (Royal Engineer) many of the young subalterns (junior officers) had come from the drawing offices of local councils, and did not know hay from a bull's foot! Nothing was available until the end of December 1939 when it was announced at the Kettering Recruiting Office that a number of construction companies' Royal Engineers were to be formed, and they called for volunteers. Amongst thousands of others I volunteered, and on January 3rd 1940 I was called to Northampton and was sworn in by a Lt. Colonel and given my three shillings, which was the daily pay for a Sapper 3rd Class.

I was given a railway travel warrant to Clacton (Butlin's holiday camp) where I reported on January 4th 1940. The camp had previously housed U Boat German prisoners of war, and they were removed to accommodate us. It was freezing and we were allocated two to a little chalet, which was wringing wet and damp with no heating. We had to sleep fully clothed and in our overcoats, which we later parcelled up and sent home. Uniforms were not issued until many days later. Owing to living under these conditions, most developed what we nominated as the 'Clacton Cough'. We were next interviewed by an officer, and as I had had the sense to take with me my night school 1st class examination certificate in building construction, and also letters of recommendation from architects and council surveyors I had worked under, he asked me why I had not applied for a commission. I told him that I had previously written to the War Office and was told that commissions must be obtained through the ranks. The officer said that this was ridiculous and he asked me to see him later when he gave me a sealed letter to be given to my OC (Officer Commanding) when I was posted to a company.

After many escapades at Butlin's camp, we were posted to companies - I to 660 General Construction Company Royal Engineers - and sent to Margate civvy (civilian) billets (lodging houses). I immediately wrote to my new OC (Officer Commanding), Captain Cross, requesting an interview as advised by my interviewing officer. On inspecting my various credentials, my smart appearance, and that I had mentioned in my letter that my father had served in the Scots Guards during the Great War (as it happened Captain Cross was a London Scots man, which was helpful), he ended the interview by stating that he could not recommend me for a Royal Engineer's Commission (for which I would have had to have taken a degree at University), but he could - if I so desired - send me to OCTU (Office Cadet Training Unit) to train for an infantry commission. My reply was that I had no desire to receive an infantry commission, but would rather have, if possible, an NCO's (Non-commissioned Office) rank. The next day I was appointed Lance Corporal (one stripe), which automatically raised me from three shillings a day (3rd class sapper) to 1st class tradesman with pay of five shillings and nine pence a day, plus a further nine pence a day for my one stripe – a total 6/6 per day (riches indeed!).

During this time, our house was sold and the furniture stored at the 'New Inn', Desborough, for the duration of the war, and Mary returned to Leicester to live with her mother, and get a job; it was a traumatic time.

CHAPTER TWO – JANUARY 1940

On the 24th of January 1940, I was drilling a section of men on Margate promenade in mid afternoon when a runner came up informing me that the Company Sergeant Major required my presence at the company office. On arriving there I was taken to Captain Cross' office, where he told me that 660 company would be going to France as part of an R.E. (Royal Engineers) Battalion, consisting of 660, 661, 662 and 663 companies R.E., named 'X Force'. The battalion's main complement of vehicles had already been dispatched, and I was to leave that evening with three drivers to Dover. I was to be in command of a huge Humber Snipe estate car, two lorries, and four motorbikes. I was told to pack my kit bag and rifle, and accompanied Captain Cross in his car to the main square of Margate while the four company's vehicles were awaiting dispatch.

I was taken to Lt. Col Knutt - the officer commanding X Force - and I was amazed to hear myself introduced to him as - and I quote – 'Colonel, this is Corporal Marlow, my senior Corporal who I would like to put in command of all the four companies' vehicles, and that the other three corporals' nine drivers of 661, 2 and 3 be placed under his command!' The Colonel readily agreed and wished me a successful voyage; cor!

Apparently, this was to be an additional convoy to the main one already dispatched. Two officers then introduced themselves to me as my convoy guides to Dover, and off we went to Dover with six inches of snow on the roads and freezing temperatures.

We arrived safely that night on Dover docks. My other three Lance Corporals, 12 drivers and I found a room on the docks with a concrete floor, and settled down to enjoy whatever sleep we could get with one blanket each. The officer guides told me that I would be boarding a ship in the morning with my vehicles bound for Dunkirk, and on Dunkirk docks a Captain Daniels would meet me, when my responsibilities would be ended, and he would take over. When boarding, I noticed a large number of ambulances being lifted on board.

We accordingly set sail on January 25th 1940, and shortly afterwards I received an order to report to the officer commanding all troops on board. He was a Major RASC (Royal Army Service Corps), who had bought 100 ambulances together with a RASC company. He told me that as I was in charge of four Humber

Snipe estate cars, eight lorries and 16 motorbikes, I had to supply him with a listed description of all vehicles together with manufacturers' numbers, chassis numbers, etc. This I did, and found him to be very helpful and good humoured.

Arriving at Dunkirk, I landed to find no Captain Daniels available, and nobody had ever heard the name! I was directed to take my convoy of vehicles to the French military barracks in Dunkirk. We stayed the night on straw on the barrack floor and had a meal, which I think was horsemeat. After consideration, I thought that my best bet would be to find the RASC Major who I found had been given an office at the barracks and parking for his 100 ambulances. I explained to him my situation, and he did some telephoning around. He was able to inform me that one of the company's men and vehicles would be going to the same destination as his, and he offered to take them with him. He also arranged that at a certain crossroads about 20 miles out of Dunkirk, his convoy would go straight on, we would turn left, and two French officer guides would take me on to my destination.

I duly met the guides and established a rapport with them by conversing in Kettering Grammar School French. After some travelling, we stopped the convoy on a road which I thought was outside a village; however, we were actually on the extreme outskirts of the city of Lille! At about 1.30pm the guides left, informing me that a British Officer would contact me at 3.00pm and take us to our destination. No one came at all, so I thought "here we go again"! I decided to walk into town after leaving instructions to my Lance Corporals and drivers not to leave their vehicles. I was in luck; I did not walk more than a mile when I came upon a notice board proclaiming that this was an R.E. depot. I found a very helpful Regimental Sergeant Major who telephoned around for me and finally came up with a slip of paper with '3 Rue De La Gare, St Andre, Lille'. He said this was the best information he could find. He told me that St Andre was a suburb of Lille, but unfortunately was on the far side.

It was now about 4.00pm, dusk, and snow was falling, so he wished me good luck getting across the large city of Lille. Arriving back at the convoy I sorted them out, and was just about to leave at 4.30pm when what happened? My two French guides returned! I showed them my slip of paper with the address and they knew nothing about it. They did ask me if the British Officer had turned up, and I told them no. They then told me to leave the convoy halted, and took me in their car to GHQ Lille. There I met a General and showed him my address slip. He telephoned around and said that he was unable to find our destination, so he said that I might just as well try St Andre.

Arriving back at the convoy, it was 5.00pm, snowing steadily; my two guides then began thinking about their dinner, and they had lost their enthusiasm. They then came up with a great idea; they would guide me to St Andre with me in my Humber Snipe following them. Then, I could return to the convoy, and bring it to St Andre.

So, we arrived at St Andre, which was the correct place anyway. The guides said "Good Luck, Au Revoir!". I then found the Company Sergeant Major, who cross-questioned me thoroughly about my exploits. When he asked me what service I had, and I told him that it was 22 days, he blew his top and shouted unintelligible bad words to the high heavens! He then marched me in to see his Colonel, who was a very nice man. He told me that my company HQ was at Nomain about 20 miles up the road. One of the companies had left that morning and the other company were billeted with him.

He told me that if I could cross Lille again, find my convoy, and return safely to St Andre, he would ensure a good hot meal and a warm billet for everyone, no matter what time. Snow was still falling - I forgot to tell you that all the French cobbled roads had a three-inch coating of solid ice - it was a bad winter. I was not thrilled with the prospect, and although my memory was not good enough to get me to the convoy, at least I had had the sense to write down the name of the road where I had left the convoy (also, someone 'up there' had been looking after me) – so off we went.

We had not travelled far when two French youths thumbed a lift; I stopped. I showed them the name of the road where I had left the convoy; they knew it, and I said that if they would guide me there, they would have a lift. Fortunately, they lived close by. I reached the convoy. I will never know how I remembered to find the way again across the great city of Lille on a snowy night complete with convoy, but I did. End of exploit.

About ten days later, the 660 company joined me at Nomain, and we settled down to work. I helped build pillboxes, block houses, etc. Among the section I was appointed to, I met and palled up with Geoff Stones, a Yorkshire man. We both made other good friends, especially at the estaminet (small café/bistro) in the village of Nomain, and on occasional visits to Lille. Sometime after I had settled down, I was Lance Corporal Guard Commander on sentry duty, on 24 hours shift. At 6.00pm, the Company Sergeant Major called and asked for me. I greeted him, and he said "you are improperly dressed!" I checked myself, and said "sorry Company Sergeant Major, but I can't see that I am!" He said "did you read company orders that are posted outside company office at 6.00pm?", and I said "no, I was on guard duty." He said "it was on orders tonight that you had been promoted to full Corporal" (2 stripes); apparently, Colonel Knutt had heard of my exploits, and at a luncheon he told Captain Cross that news of my exploits had reached him, and my initiative must be rewarded. He thanked Captain Cross for recommending me, and told him to promote me to full Corporal immediately.

Our company was made up of four sections of approximately 60 men each, with a section Sergeant (three stripes with a bomb above), a Corporal (two stripes) – both of those of my section were men in their forties – and a Lance Corporal at that time (me). Our section was billeted in a barn at a farm about the same size as our workshops at Gold Street, Desborough, the cows were cleared out, and straw was spread on the floor, on which we slept for the next three months. There was a pump from which we obtained water for ablution, and the food was poor and little. It was a very bad winter, and most mornings we woke with a layer of snow on top of our blankets.

This particular period was named the phoney war; nothing happened. Part of this – about four weeks – was enlivened by the arrival of a Coldstream Guards Sergeant, who began training, and smartened up our N.C.O's, from Lance Corporal upwards, including me. One day, we were taken to a firing range about 15 miles away. There, two feet square targets were set up 200 yards away with a 6" bull in the centre. We were given five rounds per rifle for practice, and the old sweats decided we should have a five franc sweep (150 francs to the winner, which they confidently expected to win). However, in the practice, I got 4 bulls and one inner. I thought this seemed easy and in the final shoot off I got five bulls in a two-inch circle. I collected the 150 francs prize, which surprised a good many. I realised from then on I was a naturally good shot (no false modesty).

CHAPTER THREE – MAY 1940

The phoney war ended with our entry over the Belgian border at 2.30pm on May 10th, 1940. We proceeded to our final destination, Tournai, in Belgium. We built a road and various defences. We encountered daily and intensive bombing by arrowhead formations of 27 aircrafts.

In less than 2 weeks, we were back at Nomain. On arriving there the whole company disembarked from our lorries, and formed up in ranks at our parade yard. We were given a pep talk by Colonel Knutt, and were then dismissed. We were just getting undercover, when a German aircraft appeared. He had been hedge-hopping, and immediately started machine-gunning. Luckily for us he was five minutes late, or he could have killed the lot of us. However, no-one was touched.

On the evening of May 26th we left Nomain for an unknown destination, and a number of French towns we passed through were in flames from air strikes; the Germans had complete control of the skies. En route we were ordered to dump our kit bags (mine contained a silver hairbrush, one of a pair Mary had bought us) and finally arrived at Dunkirk docks at about 10.00am on May 27th. All vehicles were immobilised and made unserviceable. We were then ordered to disperse into town, and our section found an area of grass in a square. The oil containers had already been dive-bombed, and a pall of smoke lay over Dunkirk. As we lay trying to catch up with a little sleep, suddenly squadrons of Stukas appeared and dropped bombs on all the surrounding houses in the square. Geoff Stones and I were lying at the corner of the parkland at the junction of two streets, when two bombs dropped less than two yards away at either side of the corner. The streets were all cobbled, the bombs were small, and each only made a crater about three feet across and three feet deep. The shrapnel went over the top of us, and wounded some men about thirty yards beyond us.

After this, we were ordered to take cover in the Seaman's Rest. Dunkirk was continuously bombed and machine-gunned. At about 5.00pm, we were ordered to move out (no more than six at a time), get through the town, over the canal bridge, and to the beach. We saw a number of French policemen who had been killed in the machine gunning. Arriving at the beach we were ordered to form parties of fifty to be ready for evacuation; however two destroyers arrived quickly, filled up, and left.

The parties of fifty were dispersed, as no other ships were expected. The beach was continuously bombed and machine-gunned, so we had to take whatever cover possible, which was nil.

A Navel Officer beach master was on the beach, so I approached him and asked his opinion; it was then, of course, dark. He said that as no ships were expected until the next day, it would be best to find shelter in the buildings on the promenade.

Geoff and I found a toy shop with a cellar and a concrete floor above, and settled in for the night, and we were joined by a dozen others. At 4.00am the next morning I was awakened by some shouting on the promenade, and I saw a procession of men in single file making for the 'mole'. I roused the others, and told them to follow on. The 'mole' was a walkway above the sea about 1000 yards long and three feet wide. It was pitted with bomb holes, and riddled with bullets. Two destroyers and a sloop arrived at the end of the mole. The sloop and one of the destroyers filled up and left. It was slow going, as each man had to throw his rifle down on to the deck of the ship, and then jump across and down the gap between the mole and the ship.

I was just wondering whether we would make it, as we were sitting ducks for the machine-gunning from the air, when a flight of three Hurricanes appeared and flew over us. They must have put off the Stukas, and we were the lucky ones to make it; 'him up there' again!

The destroyer was the 'Impulsive'; 1300 tonnes. The sea was as calm as a lake, we arrived at Dover three hours later, and the Impulsive returned to Dunkirk doing a shuttle. I am pleased to say that Impulsive survived the evacuation.

Stock photo of the HMS Impulsive

Arriving at Dover, we were put on a train to Barton Stacy, an R.E. camp in the south of England. I telephoned Mam and Dad; I was unable to get in touch with Mary, as she was working somewhere in Leicestershire. The next day, Mam and Dad arrived in the car. I was disappointed that Mary was not with them, but they made amends by bringing her down for the weekend. Shortly after, Geoff and I were sent to Newark where some tents had been erected on spare ground on the outskirts of the town. Mary joined me at the weekend, which we spent at the Robin Hood Hotel. We made arrangements to meet the next Sunday, but early that morning we were rounded up and put on the train for Plymouth and on to Tavistock, so Mary travelled to Newark to find me gone, as informed by the station master.

Geoff Stones' wife and her family had hired a large taxi from Normanton, Yorkshire; they had not seen Geoff since he arrived back, and Mary had the job of telling them that we had left.

So, on board the train at Newark. No breakfast, and no sign of anyone in charge, so I scoured the train until I found a 2nd Lieutenant of about 18 years old, and it seemed he was temporarily in charge but he was getting off at Sheffield. So I said "what about the men's rations?" He did not know anything about them, so I told him he better find out quickly. I never saw him again.

We arrived eventually at Bristol Railway Station at about 5.00pm. The two other Lance Sergeants who boarded with us had disappeared, so stuck with 80 plus hungry men I reported to the RTO's office (Rail Transportation Officer - there was an officer in charge of every large main railway station), and he promised to phone around. He came back to me shortly and said we were in luck. The local ladies section of the YMCA had prepared for a party of 100 men who at the last minute could not attend, so he gave me the address and said if I could march my 80 plus men to the YMCA Bristol, we would be fed. I must have had an unerring sense of direction, because we arrived safely and had an excellent meal of ham, salad, potatoes, etc., and a warm welcome.

After the meal, realising there would be no possibility of controlling 80 men belonging to probably 40 different companies, I told them that the train to Plymouth would be leaving at midnight, and to change there for Tavistock. I dare say a few absconded and made for home, but the majority turned up, and we subsequently arrived at Tavistock the next morning.

We settled in and were queuing for a midday meal at the local hall, when I spotted Mary's brother, Charles. He was in the Leicester Infantry Regiment, but I only had a few minutes chat as he was leaving, I believe, for Launceston (he was later a Japanese Prisoner of War on the 'death railway'). Some days later, I was Sergeant Guard Commander for Tavistock, and in the evening a Sapper reported to me that a Sgt Marlow wished to see me. Of course, it was my brother Norman, so I told him to join me in the guardroom, and he stayed the night. We met at lunchtime the next day at a pub, and found that Harry Hull (a childhood friend who married my wife's sister) was with him. Apparently, after I left in January 1940, they both volunteered for the same type of R.E. company as mine. Their company number was 740, I think. They had been evacuated from St. Nazaire in the South, and had been ordered aboard the Lancastria. Shortly after, they were disembarked so that all the RAF men could be together, which was a tragedy for the RAF boys, as Lancastria received a large bomb down the funnel, which sank her. Norman got away on another ship.

His company left shortly after for Launceston, and eventually spent a few months in Northern Ireland. He was promoted to

Staff Sergeant MFW, and sent to Singapore, I believe about late 1940. I didn't see him again until November 1945, at Desborough.

From Tavistock, we were sent to Perth in Scotland, being billeted at Tullock Dye works, and settled in at reasonable comfort. Food was better than we had had for many months. I was seconded from the company, and was given charge of 200 Scottish labourers. My job was to prepare the banks of the River Tay by revetting them so as to form anti-tank traps. The weather was delightful. Mary was able to obtain a week or so leave from work, and stayed at a very nice bungalow with a very kind Scottish couple in lodgings. We had a marvellous time; she was due to come again, but the company was sent to Fort William on the West Coast and she was able to visit me there for a week.

We were then posted to Kinloss Airfield on the East Coast near to the Moray Firth; it was a very large airfield. I was immediately sent to Chester on the Welsh border for the whole of November 1940 to attend an N.C.O's course in explosives and demolition. It was very interesting, and on my return I was able to give lectures to the company. We then built a number of brick pillboxes around the airfield. They were eight sided, and we had no technical tools to hand; I remembered Pythagoras's theorem, and I was able to put forward a plan for setting them out, which was adopted.

CHAPTER FOUR – FEBRUARY 1941

In February, we were all sent to Aldershot, where we prepared for embarkation to the Middle East. The night before, we entrained to Liverpool in the early hours of the 19th March 1941; ten Sappers deserted. We boarded the beautiful ship 'Andes'. Newly built by Harland and Wolff (shipbuilders in Belfast) in September 1939 I believe; 26,000 tonnes, and 26 knots per hour. After the war, she was refitted and became the popular and lovable ship R.M.S. Andes, and was later captained by Captain Fox of Lubenham, Market Harborough, a friend of my accountant and his wife Mr and Mrs Jack and Lily Smith.

We lay off the Isle of Anglesey until 23rd March 1941 while this great convoy assembled. There were 50,000 troops in 17 ships, with an escort of two battleships, six cruisers, and 12 destroyers (the biggest to date). One of the ships was RMS Georgic, with 3000 airmen aboard bound for Canada for training, guarded by one of the battleships in the mid-Atlantic. She left us as we turned due south past the Azores, and to our first port of call, Freetown, the 'white man's grave' in West Africa. We anchored off shore for four days while we refuelled.

Coming on board we were all skint; apart from the fact that we had received no pay for two weeks before boarding, the Officer in Command of the troops decided that Sergeants and below that rank should receive seven shillings per week. As half a pint of beer cost seven pence in the Sergeants' mess, we knew we were in for a miserable time. The officers and warrant officers had unlimited access to drinks.

I had been feeling very fit, exercising and boxing etc. on board. Shortly after leaving port, I developed prickly heat, which is an itchy rash, forming an eight-inch deep rash around the buttocks and abdomen. I had this for six weeks, with very little sleep!

There were no U-Boat attacks. We left Freetown for Cape Town, where half of the convoy (including us) put into port whilst the other sailed onto Durban. During the journey, we crossed the equator, and I was chosen to take part in the 'crossing the line' ceremony on April 9th 1941, as you will see on my certificate signed by the Commodore, on the next page.

The 'Crossing the Line' certificate, signed by the Commodore

Briefly, King Neptune, his Queen and Court, together with the Court Police, climbed over the side of the ship and set up court by the swimming pool, where at one end a huge ducking chair was erected. I was accused of saying that "there was no Santa Claus and the queen was an old hay bag". Then, King Neptune ordered the court police to seize me, and they dragged me to the ducking chair. There, the court barber, with his three feet long wooden razor shaved me with liberal amounts of custard and then tipped me over backwards into the pool! After a dozen or more had received similar, we then all turned on the King, Queen and Court, and threw them into the pool. It was great fun.

We docked at Cape Town for four days, which was marvellous. We were on route marches through Cape Town every morning from 10.00am to noon, back for lunch, and then on leave in Cape Town from 2.00pm till midnight. During the route marches we used to fall out for a break at about ten minutes to the hour. At one break, an old lady in her sixties, dressed in black, approached me and said "Do you come from Northamptonshire?" To this I said "yes". Then, she asked "do you know Desborough?" To this, I said "Yes I was born and bred there". Then she said "Did you know that Mr Grudgings had died?" Now, Mr Grudgings had been the headmaster during my schooling at Desborough Council School from 7 to 11 years, until I won a scholarship to Kettering Grammar School at 11 years old. Small world, eh? She was a family friend, and had corresponded with them.

Cape Town gave us a very warm welcome, which was appreciated by all of us, as it had been touch and go as to whether we would have been allowed to land. The previous convoy to ours had contained the Australian sixth division, which we were told consisted of many roughnecks and hobos who had, for fun, jumped on the horse drawn brewers' wagons and tapped all the barrels of beer, picked up an Austin Seven car, carried it into Barclays Bank, and placed it on the counter. Also, it was not deemed to be safe for ladies out in the evening. Parties of Methodist Chapel ladies kindly took a number of us, when we arrived ashore, up to the railway station in Adderley Street by train to Simonstown, where the train stopped on the beach; we changed into swimming gear lent to us so we could have a swim. We were later taken back to Wynberg, which was on the way back to Cape Town, and were given a splendid meal, and afterwards we were taken to a dance laid on for us.

On the last evening, I was with another Sergeant when a young man who turned out to be an architect stopped us, and invited us to dinner at his house at the top of Table Mountain. On arriving, it was the cook's evening off, and his wife, of course, did no cooking, so I saved the day and volunteered to cook ham and eggs for all of us. He drove us back down Table Mountain to arrive at the ship at midnight.

So, goodbye to dear Cape Town. I later found that an R.E. company ship broke down, and that they had to stay in Cape Town for three months. Some people have all the luck!

CHAPTER FIVE – MAY 1941

We arrived at Port Tewfik at the south end of the Suez Canal on May 5th 1941. The voyage from Liverpool to Egypt had taken 49 days. We were then moved by train to Beni Yusef camp, 15 miles from Cairo, and five miles from the Pyramids at Mena. It was 117.5 degrees Fahrenheit; a heat wave for Egypt. We had been bound for Greece, which fell before we got there, so we were given two weeks to acclimatise, during which we were at liberty in the afternoons to visit Cairo and the pyramids. We enjoyed exploring the Great Pyramid, the Sphinx, etc.

Exploring the pyramids in Egypt

We were then sent to Haifa in Palestine, where we stayed for two or three weeks until the Syria campaign opened up and we were attached to the Australian 7th division to build bridges over the Litani and Damour rivers.

Syria, 1941

All the trained peacetime Royal Engineers' companies were down in Abbysinia (Ethiopia) where they were desperately needed because of the terrain of the country. They were scraping the barrel to send us to Syria, but we duly went in on Mary's birthday, June 8th 1941. Our first objective was the Litani River, a fast flowing river over which we were required to build a stock span bridge (Bailey bridges were not in use until later). We had no training whatsoever on building bridges, but that did not bother us.

Using stock span bridges meant launching two huge girders on RSJs (Rolled Steel Joists) from a launching pad on the home side, with an engaging steel arm bolted to the far ends, with a wheel on the far end. The angle at which to place the launching arm was a matter of sensible judgement. Unfortunately, we had a Lieutenant (who I believe had served in India) who was totally incompetent; when I saw the angle at which the launching arm was bolted, I told him as Sergeant in charge of the men that it would never engage the far bank. He overrode my objections. There we were, about 15 men sitting on the girder, counter balancing like a lot of Charlies; the launching arm never engaged the far bank, having been bolted on at an angle three feet higher than required. We, girder and all, finished up in the river – oh calamity! Three ton lorries had to be fixed together with towing ropes between each one and lashed to the end of the girder, before dragging it back out. Back to square one!

The launching arm had to be unbolted and fixed at an angle I had suggested in the first place, and eventually after working 20 hours without a break, we completed the bridge. June in Lebanon in 1941 was over 100 degrees, and the book says that this type of bridge should have taken a quarter of the time.

We then set off up the Saida Road, and apart from snakes getting familiar (we slept on the ground with one blanket and a waterproof cape), some sniping, and being shelled at point blank range by a Vichy French destroyer sailing off shore, it was fairly uneventful. We finally reached the River Damur with a two span stone bridge about 50 feet above the river, and one of the spans about 100 feet long having been destroyed.

Our section of 60 men had dwindled to myself and fifteen others. The rest had gone down with malaria and dysentery. The Vichy General Dentz came driving through the banana groves in his staff car to sue for peace. A very qualified R.E. army troop company, complete with all manor of vehicles and bridge building equipment arrived. They commenced operations for a probable two weeks job. My gang was given the job of damming the river and excavating into the riverbed to form a foundation for a massive fifty feet high steel stanchion back to Tyre in Lebanon.

The next morning, after getting on the lorry with my kit, I promptly collapsed with a temperature of 105 degrees. I was sent by ambulance to a casualty clearance station, and during the night I was continually bathed on my head and neck by a kind orderly. He had red hair, and funnily enough, just after the war I went to an Alamein reunion up in London, and we were given bunks in a former air raid shelter. It was on my way back on the tube that I met a red haired fellow (who had also been at the reunion) who I thought I recognised, and I asked him if he had been in the RAMC (Royal Army Medical Corps) at number 21 casualty clearing station in June 1941. He had, and of course he was the kind orderly who had attended me; coincidence!

I was then taken by ambulance to Sarafan hospital near Tel Aviv. I was kept there for a week with all the symptoms of malaria, with a 105 degree temperature. I was extremely well looked after, but although I had umpteen blood tests, they never found the parasite in my blood. I am sure I had 'sand fly' fever, which had all the same symptoms as malaria because I went down with the same symptoms after I returned from an anti-malaria course for 3 weeks when I rejoined my 660 company after convalescing at el-Arish after hospital. At convalescence camp I met Gerard Pace from Desborough, who was convalescing after an appendix operation.

I rejoined my company and on the night I got back I saw, on company orders, an invitation to apply for Probationer Staff Sergeant Foreman of Works with engineer services. I applied, and was accepted. I then had a three month waiting period before leaving, and during that time, as I previously mentioned, I was sent on a three week course to Sarafan Hospital, Tel Aviv, which we used as a headquarters and daily went out on buses visiting Jerusalem, Bethlehem, Jericho, Nazareth, River Jordon, etc., which were breeding grounds for the female anopheline mosquito. It was tremendously interesting, and I learned all about preventative action to be taken against the malarial mosquito, taking eggs from mountain streams and retaining the mosquitoes in test tubes. I did well on the course, which was attended by about 20 officers and sergeants from different units. I was able to put my knowledge to good use when I returned to 660 Company.

CHAPTER SIX – JANUARY 1942

In January 1942, I left Syria, bound for the R.E. base depot at Moascar on the Suez; I was there to await posting. Three of us left at 4.00am to the sound of the Makhzen calling the faithful to prayer, then went by lorry to a railway, and onto Damascus where we stayed the night. Then, we went across the plain of Sinai to Haifa in Palestine, and finally to Moascar, Egypt, on the Suez. We were then stuck there for six weeks waiting for the desert train to take us up to Sidi Barrani, and during that time Singapore fell, and I had to presume that my brother Norman was 'in the bag'. Strangely enough, I did receive a short printed card from Norman some months later informing us that he was at least alive. I never heard anything after that, and I now know why.

We arrived at Sidi Barrani, which was just a point on a map in the desert together with a battalion of the Durham Light Infantry of the famous 50th Division, in a usual dusty storm which lasted 48 hours; it was impossible to see anything. We happened to find a small tent, which was some shelter. No-one seemed to know the whereabouts of our new unit, so next morning we were loaded in threes on 15 CWT (hundred weight) lorries loaded with three inch mortar bombs bound for Tobruk. At that time, the Luftwaffe had command of the skies, so we were subject to some strafing on our night stops. The trick was to dig a grave some two feet down, so one could be below ground for some protection. Tobruk was an unhealthy place with intermittent air raids. The allowance of one bottle of water per man daily always tasted salty. We did at last find our unit more by accident that design.

I woke up next morning ready to commence duties and found that my skin was yellow from head to foot. My long travels around the desert sleeping rough had caused me to develop yellow jaundice. I saw the Medical Orderly and he ordered me to a tented hospital. The care was doses of salts and little to eat, and normally lasted for three weeks. After eight days I had regained my normal colour and was feeling reasonably well, so I asked the doctor if I could be discharged, as it was important for me to commence my three months probation for Staff Sergeant; however, matron played hell and said that none of her patients for yellow jaundice had been discharged under three months. I pointed out that I had been wandering around the desert for three weeks previously looking for my unit, and during that time had symptoms of no appetite and was passing dark brown coloured urine, which was now clear. I was allowed to join my unit.

The 8th army had retreated to El Alamein, so that area I was in was a bask area approximately 26 miles from Alexandria. I reported to the DCRE (Deputy Commander, Royal Engineers) who was in command of the area, and he told me that the fullest use of native labour was to be used. He told me that my knowledge and experience had been noted, but I would have to show that I could get results personally. I was then placed under the Garrison Engineer Captain Buchannan, who had been previously a section officer 1st Lieutenant with 660 company. He knew all about me, but although he had been in the same company I had never met him, as he was in a different section. He told me he was pleased to have me with him, and I found him very friendly and good to work with.

My programme was to produce three landing grounds; I believe they were LG 97, 98, and 99, from which the South African air force operated Kittihawk fighters and light bombers, the RAF had Bolton and Baltimore Light Bombers for attacking German and Italian troops beyond El Alamein, and the RAF had Wellington Bombers for attacking German convoys across the

Mediterranean. I was on LG 97 one morning in June 1942, when Winston Churchill landed to inspect the troops. I was only a yard away when he stepped out of the aircraft.

I was given 400 Arab labourers to handle, so I quickly learned to count and speak a little Arabic. As the South African air force needed more permanent depot buildings, bricks were needed quickly. I was shown an area where a few hundred bricks were made. The bricks were produced as in biblical days out of sand and water mixed into mud, with cut straw or chaff called 'tibbin' as reinforcement, and laid out to bake in the sun. Luckily, at the R.E. compound I found several hundred two feet by two feet concrete paving slabs, so I had six platforms laid on the ground each to take 1000 bricks (9" by 4" by 3"), 6000 in all. I then got the employing officer of native labour to hire me 100 native women who were experienced in making bricks with a wooden frame each the size of a brick. The male native labourers were employed in mixing the mud and tibbin for the bricks.

So, within a few days I was producing 6000 bricks per day, the method being as follows; bricks were made during the day, left to set and harden (remember, the normal temperature was 110 degrees Fahrenheit), cleared from the platforms and carted away and so on. It made Captain Buchannan lift his eyebrows!

For my third job, I was taken to a mound in the desert, which was full of rock. I was able to obtain a very large petrol compressor with four jackhammers, with the native to use the jackhammers with which holes were drilled eight feet deep and one and a half inches in diameter every 6 feet. Every day I blew the rock, which was loaded and carried away in lorries for road making.

I had never used any explosive since my month's course at Chester in November 1940, but my memory was good. I obtained a large supply of Amonal in boxes – a grey powder, very volatile. The bottom of a hole was filled with Amonal explosive, and the rest of the hole was filled with damp sand, which I tapped until solid with an eight foot by one and a half inch wooden rod. I exploded it by using flexible fuse (instantaneously detonating), and had a gun cotton primer tied to the ends and then across the tops of the holes. I joined them together with a 10 feet run of FID (Fuse Instantaneous Detonation) with a gun cotton primer at each, and finally with a detonator and two feet of ordinary fuse for me to light, which gave me two minutes to get out of the way. In this manner, I could blow 70 cubic yards of rock each time, so it was not long before I had a quarry.

A Northamptonshire man, Alfie Barratt, also from 660 company, who was with another Garrison Engineer on different projects, was promoted at the same time as myself to Staff Sergeant Foreman of works (a war office appointment), and as we had had no leave since leaving England, we were given seven days leave to Cairo, which was very enjoyable. During this time, the 9th Australian Division came down from Syria, and the 51st Highland Division came out from England to reinforce El Alamein.

Having rejoined our ORE after leave, everything went back to routine. I had the three landing grounds under my supervision, and it gave me some satisfaction every morning to see the first flight of the day – 18 Boston and Baltimore light bombers covering the troops at El Alamein together with Kittihawk fighters. We still had the usual bombing and strafing, particularly at night or before dawn on a waning moon.

CHAPTER SEVEN – OCTOBER 1942

October 23rd 1942 came, commencing with the Tremain Artillery barrage, which lit up the skies for miles around. The Battle of El Alamein was conducted by highly trained Royal Engineer field squadrons, clearing the minefields to make a passage for the tanks, infantry and artillery, and it was not until the battle was over and Rommers in retreat that we followed up. My duties consisted of following the 8th Army of which we were a part, going out alone in my 15cwt truck with empty 40 gallon petrol drums in the back, and a prismatic compass. I was required to find flat areas of desert on a 330 degree bearing, 1500 yards long by 50 yards wide, clearing them and putting up three 40 gallon drums at each corner for markings. When ready (it only took a day or two), they accommodated Spitfires and Hurricanes etc. for covering forward troops.

We reached a former German airfield at Agedabia, which was quite small, and as the 8th Army were using it to air-evacuate wounded from the front, I was given the job of extending it. It was there that I again met up with Gerald Page from Desborough who was with an air evacuation for wounded unit RAMC. As no auto graders were available, they sent me a huge tractor and a "box scraper", which had wheels 10 feet high and two feet wide. Work went on with extending the airfield until one day there was a bang. It was my usual practise to walk all over the airfield, and at times I walked by the side of the huge wheels of the scraper, checking that a correct cut was being taken. However, on this particular day I was about 100 yards away from the tractor and box scraper when there was a tremendous explosion. On running over, I found that a teller mine had blown two of the scraper's wheels to smithereens. The airfield had been checked for mines before operating, but the Germans had buried a teller mine set deep, and the pressure to cause the explosion had been set so that ordinary vehicles would not explode it, and they obviously hoped to catch one of the DC3 aircraft evacuating the wounded. Apparently, the heavy tractor went over the teller mine but did not explode it, and it was not until the huge wheels of the box scraper went over it that it exploded. As the tractor and the scraper were both long vehicles, the tractor driver was unhurt, except for being somewhat dazed, and nobody else was near or hurt.

We then carried on following the army until we reached Misurata in Tripolitania, which had an airfield and also another airfield and port called Misurata Marina. My first job was maintenance of the two airfields, so I recruited all the Bedouin Arabs of the village - about 200 men. I formed them into four groups of 50 each with a 'rais' or foreman over each. I had to issue them with sticks of cardboard with their numbers thereon, as I was also responsible for getting them paid their wages. The Bedouin are very independent, and although their wages were extremely poor, I was strict with them and they respected me. I was further helped by the DID (the unit issuing rations) who contacted me and asked if I could use any warranty-expired army biscuits which had passed their sell by date and would otherwise be destroyed, dozens and dozens of boxes, the answer to a maiden's prayer. I was then regarded as the most popular 'Bash showish' (phonetic), as any good work done was rewarded with biscuits, which they crushed up and mixed with chilli. Yum Yum in Arabic!

I was then joined with a Captain Garrison Engineer, another Staff Sergeant MFW, a Corporal Assistant, and an office clerk. The Captain and Corporal worked together, and the new Staff Sergeant worked with me.

The RAF, with a Wing Commander in command, had their officers' mess in Misurata, of which our Captain GE became a member, and they had unlimited gin. The Wing Commander often had jobs that wanted doing, and he passed them on to our Captain. He in turn would ring me up in the evening to give me instructions to be carried out the next morning. For instance, I was informed that an RAF officer would pick me up early the next morning to show me two different routes up a nearby mountain, where RAF equipment must be taken to the top and made to work by 5.00pm. Both routes needed work doing, so I chose the best route and then had a word with two of my gangs, informing them that they would have to work hard and fast with their picks and shovels, and that if we were successful, lots of warranty-expired biscuits would be provided. We carried out the work successfully and on time for which our Captain received a pat on the back from Wing Commander.

Another time, I had a call from the Captain in the evening to say that an object had been washed ashore at Misurata marina, and as it was close to the RAF buildings and might be a mine or explosive, Wing Commander mentioned it to Captain, who volunteered to remove it. Captain picked me up in his 15cwt next morning, and off we went. I asked him why the RAF armourers were not doing the job for which they had the equipment and experience. He poo-pooed this, and we duly parked next to the object. I got into the back of the truck, sat on the wheel arch, and cradled my arms. He took a deep breath, lifted it up and placed it into my arms, jumped in, and we shot off about two miles along the shore where we blew the thing up with a gun cotton slab, primer, and detonator. After all this to-do, it was not a mine or even an explosive. The RAF men watched and duly applauded our antics.

Another time, I had a call from him to say that he and the Corporal had constructed a converted tower about 30 feet high, and he said that an Ames Radar vehicle weighing about six tons was to be got up on top the next day. As I had never seen the tower before or seen any plan, I asked "why me?" He said that as I was the Senior Staff Sergeant Foreman of Works, he thought that the work would be better in my hands. I enlisted the other Staff Sergeant to give me a hand.

As Captain had no ideas for carrying out the work, I suggested that he see Wing Commander and borrow a winch truck with stout ropes motorised. The tower was square topped, with two wing ramp walls built at 45 degrees, 15 inches wide, on which the six ton wheeled vehicle could be hauled up.

Away we went with an RAF Sergeant in charge of the winch lorry and ropes, and with the other Staff Sergeant and myself each crawling up the ramps behind the vehicle in the heat of 100 degrees plus, hoping that no ropes would snap. By a hint of an inch or two at a time, we reached the platform, and of course found that whoever had planned the thing had not realised that you can't get a six ton vehicle from a 45 degree ramp to a square flat platform, so the thing stuck fast on its chassis.

Early afternoon and we were still stuck, and along came Captain enquiring why we had not finished the job. We made certain caustic remarks about the planning of the tower etc., and being fortified by his luncheon gin he went up the ramp with a hammer and chisel and started hammering away at the point where it was stuck. It was obvious to us that this was absolutely stupid and told him so, but he knew better, and after he had removed a few inches of masonry the vehicle moved and trapped his leg below the knee; oh calamity! We managed to haul the vehicle off of his leg and sent for the ambulance. They put him on a stretcher and he lay on it awaiting removal. As he left he called "Carry on staff!" The famous words of a wounded hero?

It was now dark, so we got the RAF Sergeant to leave his truck for the night with the winches locked. We then left the site, had a meal, got our heads together, and came up with the idea of sawing some planks we had (15" long), so that we could build them about 12" high under the back wheels of the vehicle. We did this the next day, and we both had a hair-raising time of putting our ideas into action, which worked and we completed the job. If the slightest thing had gone wrong we would have been swept off those ramps like flies!

I was walking around the Misurata airfield one day, and on passing the RAF operations room I ran into a newly promoted Group Captain - the overall boss. He said "you must be Staff Marlow in charge of the airfield." On being questioned I told him that I had produced a number of landing grounds, and he asked me if I had ever been up in an aircraft to see what my markings looked like. I said "no", and he said "we will soon remedy that, I will order one of my flight lieutenant pilots to take you up." I did not meet anyone for a week when I at last ran into a New Zealand

Flight lieutenant, who of course said "are you Staff Marlow"?, to which I confessed, and he said "Groupie told me a week ago to take you up, and as we are well met I am taking a test flight up in 10 minutes time". So, off we went to the plane, which was a Beaufort Torpedo Light Bomber. The pilot and his wireless operator were in full flying kit, parachutes strapped onto their backs and all. I pointed to his parachute and said "Where's mine"? The pilot told me confidentially - and I quote - "I would rather crash land than bail out any day"! This hardly reassured me when a young pilot officer about 21 years old strolled up and said to the flight lieutenant pilot "can I come up for a spin"? So off we all flew. He gave me a good flight of both airfields, which was interesting, diving from several thousand feet down to 20 feet above the waves. I must say I enjoyed it.

These were just odd incidents on top of the usual daily workload and this continued until the end of the campaign in Tunisia. Our CRE Colonel Cubitt, delighted to be up the front, and the first man into Sfax and Knfidaville, had his luck run out; whilst in his staff car he was taken prisoner by a German patrol and was flown back to Italy.

The desert campaign finished with the capture of Rommel's army by the 8th and 1st armies by the end of March 1943. Routine continued at a more leisurely rate and there was talk and rumour of where we should move to next. Our Captain thought that he would be chosen for the next show and we would probably be left behind, but it turned out somewhat differently.

Later, I was the only one to receive orders from CRE HQ to leave everything and be ready to join a lorry convoy, to pick me and my kit up for the seven days journey. Back to Cairo the next day, all my Bedouin turned out to see me off in great style. I left feeling that I had made some contribution. There was a rumour that we were to be given leave, but on arriving at GHE Cairo, a major who had left our CRE some months earlier came out not to welcome us, but to tell us that no leave would be granted and we were to carry on another 40 miles to Kasasin to carry out alterations to our vehicles for a sea landing invasion.

We were admitted to a warrant office and Sergeant's mess at this base depot, where we were to enjoy two months of clean and comfortable living after two years of rough stuff, when the only drinks we got was two bottles of beer each Christmas. The stewards at the club apologised for having no beer but they had unlimited gin and ice for gin slings, which we duly appreciated.

I then found that I had been posted together with Alfie Barratt to a section comprising a Major who I had not previously met, a Captain (Garrison Engineer) who I had known as a lieutenant in 660 company, and also a young lieutenant who Alfie and I remembered, and who as luck would have it was a pal of my previous Captain who had been left behind. There was no Warrant Officer, but I acted in that position as I was Senior Staff Sergeant, with Alfie Barratt as my second with various assistants, drivers and officer's batmen. We were part of 231 Assault Brigade commanded by Brigadier Urquart (later a Major General at Arnhem), a battalion each of Dorsets, Hamps and Devons who had arrived from Malta with all the auxiliaries of Royal Engineers, Field Squadrons, Signals, RASC, etc.

One day, Brigadier Urquart asked our Major if he thought his men (us) could march 20 miles in a day in case of no transport. Our Major detailed his Captain to take all of us on a 10 mile route march the next day along a tarmac road with temperatures of at least 110 degrees at 2.00pm (the hottest part of the day), carrying equipment and haversacks.

Now, Alfie Barratt and I were both about 25 years old, carried no surplus weight, and were as fit as hard living and sparse food can make you. The Captain was about the same age, but was a little overweight with an arrogant manner, and all he carried was a walking stick. We set off for five miles down the road and five miles return. I marched in front together with the Captain. I set a good rate for the first five miles, but on the return I increased my pace, some of the older men dropped out, and Captain, who was sweating profusely, at last said "take your bloody time"! I eased a little, but we got back safely with Captain in a vile humour. However, no mention of a route march was ever made again.

CHAPTER EIGHT – JULY 1943

Alfie and I had examined our three officers, and we were not impressed, but we would, as always, obey the commands. It was decided that 231 Assault Brigade would board three liners at a port south of Suez for a 400 mile trip down the red sea to practice assault landing with boats holding 34 men. The sea was too rough for landing, and we had to travel back 300 miles before we found a suitable landing similar to that we were expecting to attack.

Everything went well until we got ashore. Alfie and I had not been given any instructions; the Captain said that our Lieutenant would be leading us ashore to where we had to report. What happened? Our Lieutenant could not find his way and he was soon asking private soldiers the way. We soon found ourselves stepping over infantrymen prone on the ground firing in mock battle, and we could hear Brigadier Urquart giving battle orders to units on the phone. His aid de camp saw us, and our Lieutenant asked him where to go. The aid reported to the Brigadier, and then we heard an angry bellow, "tell them to get the bloody hell out of here"! So ended our chaotic mock invasion.

We re-embarked and reached Port Said; we left Port Said in our three ships in a large convoy on July 1st 1943, bound, as we now knew, for Sicily. 231 Assault Brigade had the orders to capture 1000 yards of beach initially.

On Friday 9th July, we had the most horrendous storm in the Mediterranean, but we reached a point 100 miles short of Sicily at 6.00pm. We remained stationary until we sailed again, and reached a point about 10 miles from Sicily by midnight. I was on duty on deck and watched two boat loads of 30 infantry men and four RE to each boat; all had blackened their hands and faces carrying Bandalore Torproofs (lengths of explosives) for blowing up barbed wire defences. An infantry Captain was in command and he haranged his troops for a few minutes, ending up with "Remember Malta Lads." They disembarked down the side of our ship at 2.00am, and 45 minutes later I saw a red and green light go up signalling that the beach was secured and the main body could commence disembarking into the assault boats.

We disembarked just after dawn with the artillery, 25 powders, and small collapsible mountain guns. Somebody was carrying a radio, and on the 6.00am morning news I heard the reporter say that our troops were landing in Sicily.

The objective of our section was Pachino airfield. In reaching there we found a pioneer company fresh out from England checking for mines. As the bigwigs had been prepared for 50% casualties, there were many assorted troops about. The opposition was lower than expected, and we pressed on, preparing new air strips. Fighting lasted a few weeks and the Italians surrendered. Our section was broken up. I do not know what happened to the officers, but Alfie Barratt was in the Salerno landings in Italy, which was rough. I joined up with a Major who had been a bitumen representative and a Captain from REME (Royal Corp of Electrical and Mechanical Engineers).

We three had been chosen to go to Ragusa, Sicily, where the huge Bitumen mines of the ABC form were situated. The area was covered in sandstone rock, which was naturally impregnated with Bitumen, and was easily obtained by driving with hand augers and inserting small explosive charges. A huge quarry had been formed, probably 100 feet deep with a row of say 12 large hammer machines along the top of the quarry, into which the rock was fed and the machines hammered the rock into fine grey powder. The powder was funnelled down to the bottom of the quarry where I had my tipping lorries waiting for the powder to be loaded directly into them.

The Major had an office and telephone, responsible for admin. The REME Captain got all the hammer machines working in a few days and was then able to leave for other works. I was in charge of production and haulage of the powder to the local railway station. A Corporal was sent to me as my assistant, and the Americans, who had landed in the South of Sicily, sent me a team of six tipper lorries with drivers and a Sergeant in charge of them. The object of this exercise was as follows; the American Air Force at Gela and Victoria needed to have two large airfields with hard all-weather runways ready and operating for the coming autumn/winter of 1943/4.

The American Engineers levelled the land with their huge machines, and I had to produce all the Bitumen powder, and then deliver two goods train loads of 20/10 ton trucks to the railway station; these received and dispatched every day. The American Engineers also supplied me with a mechanical grab for loading. The tipping lorries formed a mound of powder so that the grab could fill open trucks, and as they sent whatever was available – sometimes closed trucks – when the powder was funnelled into paper sacks like cement sacks at the quarry and delivered to the station, the American Engineers unloaded the powder at their end and their machines spread it three inches thick onto their prepared ground, and then rolled it with 10 ton motor rollers, and there you had the required all-weather runways.

The Major said that he would recommend me for promotion to WO2 (Warrant Officer, 2nd class), similar to Company Sergeant Major. This did not materialise, as many Staff Sergeants and WO2's had been sent to Sicily and Italy from England and the British 1st Army, as well as the 8th Army, and promotion was based on seniority.

The Major and I went next to Bari, and then to Barletta in Italy, where a new section was formed by the addition of two Captains, one Lieutenant, and two Staff Sergeant MFW who had arrived from England. We had quite a large area to cover.

We took over several schools and converted them into seven ward/30 bed hospitals; say 210. The work generally was construction and maintenance. I was given a motorbike for my daily travel, which was about 130 miles.

It was on one of these trips that I found Jack Coe, a previous friend of mine who will be reaching 90 this year *[in 2004, the time of writing]*. He had written to me earlier, so I know what artillery battery he was with; it was a very pleasant meeting. During my stay in Barletta, I had under my supervision a large Italian parachutist barracks with my office at the entrance. At about 5.00pm one evening, the 3rd parachute battalion arrived and marched in, headed by their Regimental Sergeant Master WO1 RMS Lord, a previous Guards' Sergeant Major and a noted disciplinarian.

I also knew that Mary's younger brother Sid was a Lance Corporal with them. In the last squad marching through the entrance was young Sid, so I went out and tracked him down, had a chat with him, and invited him to my billet in town. He duly arrived at about 7.30pm, and we had a couple of bottles of vino until late when I asked him if he had to be back at a certain time; he had, and he left.

I saw Sid the next morning, and he told me he had been out on a charge for arriving late back to barracks; apparently, he climbed over the wall and landed at the feet of RMS Lord. I decided to visit RMS Lord later at his office. I told him that I was in charge of the barracks and that it was my fault that my young brother-in-law had stayed out late, as we had not seen each other for nearly four years. He told me that he had not put Sid on a charge and that it must have been some other warrant officer. He told me to forget all about it and young Sid would hear no more about it. What a nice man! If you had seen him drilling the battalion!!

The parachutist barracks was later converted into a hospital.

CHAPTER NINE – JULY 1944

Come July, and our Major left and was replaced by a younger man. We then moved up north until we reached Poggibonsi, which was about 20 miles from Florence. There we received the news that we would be taking over Florence. I was chosen to be the agent to cover the whole of Florence's Builders' Merchants sanitary ware shops and any stockist of materials. I had a very large blown-up map with all the above thereon plotted, so that I could travel the area on my motorbike and put my marker on anything I felt necessary.

As we expected to be a week or more in the woods of Poggibonsi, it gave us all the time to prepare for the takeover of Florence. I studied my maps daily and felt fully capable and excited to get to Florence. We had time for other things; for instance, one of the area Command Officers gave a piano recital including the Warsaw Concerto on a piano, which they had borrowed on the way up. On our lorry, we carried 2/40 gallon empty petrol barrels with lids on each to form ovens, and I built a large field oven using fine soil in lieu of sand, with a bag of cement we had brought along with plenty of stone lying about locally.

A RASC driver of our lorry was a good cook, and with some beef, vegetables etc. we had bought with us, he cooked the best Sunday dinner we had had for years on my speciality field oven.

In August 1944, we set out for Florence and reached the River Arno, which flows in the valley between the ranges of hills. About four miles before we entered from the south, we passed batteries of 25 founders who were busy firing at the German 88mm gun batteries situated at the heights of Fiesole above the opposite bank of the Arno. This was called "counter battery fire". The Germans had destroyed all of the beautiful bridges across the Arno except the Ponte Vecchio, upon which were built goldsmith shops, but they had covered the bridge about 30 feet high with rubble, interspersed with mines and booby traps. The British Royal Engineer Bridging Companies decided to leave the Ponte Vecchio for future clearance and built – under fire from the German 88mm guns – three Bailey bridges. The centre bridge built next to Ponte Vecchio was built in place of Ponte Trinita - where Dante met Beatrice, the extreme east bridge in place of Ponte Fero, and the extreme west bridge in place of Ponte Vitoria.

My section was billeted in an American owned villa on the Viale Michelangelo, which was near a water point, and constantly attracted shellfire. One morning, we had 16 shells exploding in our back garden, so after that I decided that the upper light of the sash windows be left down back and front so that if any shell wished to pass through the villa, it could do so without breaking the glass – which of course was strictly true!

It took the next six weeks for the Germans to be driven out of Florence. During that time, I engaged myself successfully scouring Florence. On occasion, I found myself passing a camouflaged procession of tanks waiting in the streets prior to action, when a large tank sergeant would jump out and ask me where the hell I thought I was going, and on being told, he would inform me that should I go round the jolly corner, I would get my 'B head blown off!' I used to pass and re-pass over the Ponte Trinita, and between 5.00pm and 6.00pm he always used to send several random shells over to try to help me on my way.

When most of the city was taken and the command structure had established itself in the main square, Piazza Vittorio Emanuele (later becoming Piazz della Repubblica), we took over the top floor of the Pensione Pendini for our section. Pensione Pendini was situated on the corner of Piazza della Republica and the Via Strozzi. On the triumphal archway over the Via Strozzi's entrance into the square, we established our WO's and Sergeants' mess. We had at last reached the epitome of comfort after nearly four years of efforts.

As it was over a year since I had leave in Cairo, I was given seven days leave to Rome, where we stayed in a transit camp, and for the first four days a 50 seater bus took us round all the antiquities. I also climbed up to the golden ball at the top of St Peters. I was then able to climb up to the dome in the Duomo, and also Grottos Campanile, which was 450ft high.

However, after a month's paradise, one of the Captains and myself were sent to Livorno, presumably to assist an ordinance depot. There was little for us to do, and Livorno was the lousiest dump imaginable. Every house had either been bombed or filled with booby traps. After about five weeks of purgatory, we returned to the section in Florence. The two other Staff Sergeants, who were aged in their mid-thirties, were having a marvellous time turning hotels into rest and leave hostels.

In November, a job was given to our DCRE, Major 5th Army, at San Ferdinando, about 30 miles from Florence. They had taken over a huge abandoned factory, about 500 feet long by about 100 feet in depth, roofed, and with two concrete suspended floors forming ground, 1st, and 2nd floors. No lifts, no stairways, and no doors or windows. The project was for the site to be ready to accommodate 5000 soldiers as a transit camp so that reinforcements were always available for 5th army. Who did the CRE choose? Me, because of my experience in the Middle East, and in Sicily. One of our Captains took me over to San Ferdinando, showed me the job, and told me to get on with it.

I was given authority to recruit the whole of the male population of San Ferdinando. A platoon of infantry, with their own officer, were handed over to me, from whom I hoped to find the odd carpenter or bricklayer from civvy street. There were ample supplies of building sand, planks, scaffolding and bricks on site.

My first headache was what to do about windows; cement was available from HQ Florence, but windows were a problem because I knew that there were none available in the area and there was no chance of getting any specifically made to fit the openings left in the building. However, I remembered that I had seen at least 100 fly-screens in stock at HQ Florence. They were comprised of fine metal gauze stretched over light wood frames about 4ft by 4ft, so I decided to put two frames into each large window opening and brick up the remaining space with bricks laid in cement mortar, 4ft wide. This achieved light, ventilation, and - with the weather not being cold and time being short - some degree of comfort. The infantry platoon managed to erect several sets of stairs using planks and scaffolding. During the time I was on the site, no Officer or any member of Florence HQ visited me. When I was almost finished, our Captain called to see me and to say "well done Staff, I would not be surprised to see you decorated with the BEM!!" (British Empire Medal)

I stayed until the end of 1944, and in January 1945, a complete CRE comprising Lieutenant Colonels Majors, Captains, Lieutenants, WO2's, and Staff Sergeants descended on the site and built themselves nissen huts galore to form a complete HQ. I returned to Florence to find that the length of years that the army had to stay abroad had gone down from five to four years and six months. The RAF were already down to three years. This meant that I would be due to return home in July 1945.

CHAPTER TEN – MAY 1945

In view of my expected return to England in a few months time, we had sent to us a Warrant Officer 1st Class - two ranks above me – to take over the section from me (Senior Staff Sergeant). This was ironic, as I had had charge of the section for the past two years without promotion to WO2, and now we had a WO1.

The war had ended on 8th May 1945, and things were now easier, so much so that I was even invited to become the Education Officer for the section to keep the men occupied. The WO1 realised that he had only been sent to us to fill the gap which would be left by my leaving, and he had no intention of rocking the boat. He told me to take things easy, and that as he had brought his tennis racquet with him - and if I could borrow a racquet - he and I would play tennis each afternoon on the municipal courts, which we did. There was also plenty of lovely red vermouth available, which we duly appreciated!

The two Staff Sergeants who had come from England directly to Italy were still with us. Whilst one of them was a light drinker, the elder one was tiddled up every night, and on the night before I was scheduled to travel to Naples for repatriation, he climbed out of the mess windows, 50 feet above the Via Strozzi, and edged himself along the ledge to my bedroom to say goodbye. I heard him shouting and opened my window - it was 11.00pm – I saw him coming and grabbed him as he reached my window, and I hauled him inside. So I left my lovely Florence next morning without mishap!

Arriving at Naples, I found that 25 or 26 groups for demobilization had landed there together. These were large groups. I was in No 26, and there were too many for the transit camp to handle, so about 600 of us were sent to Salerno rest camp, which was on the beach and had a large outdoor cinema, showers etc.

There were no ships available to get us home, so the powers that be ordered several squadrons of RAF Lancaster four Engine Bombers to strip out their armament and fly us back to England, 20 to each plane. So we took off from Pomigliano airport in brilliant hot sunshine on 7th August 1945, arriving at Glatton airfield 10 miles from Peterborough, late afternoon, in cold heavy rain.

One highlight of the trip; the mid-upper turret gunner of my plane invited me to take his place for 30 minutes so that I could see what France looked like from the air.

Arriving at Glatton airfield, we drew blankets from the store and were given beds in a nissen hut. We were given a meal in the evening, and as there was absolutely nothing to do until we would be put on the train to Halifax, Yorkshire, the next morning we decided to get on a bus to Peterborough, which we understood was 10 miles away. The conductors took one look at our medal ribbons and refused to take the monies for our fares. When we got off the bus an elderly man greeted us, and said that there were only two pubs open and only one had beer, so he led us to it.

I was able to telephone home, which was answered by Mary as she was at Gold Street for the weekend, as she often was. Apart from the usual greetings that I was looking forward to seeing her again, I had to say that we would still not see each other until I arrived back from Halifax in several days time.

From Halifax, we were sent home after several days for a months leave. Arriving home, it is sad to say that we were both in for a shock, and found that we were strangers. Mary and I had started going steadily together from Christmas 1936, aged 19 years, got engaged a year later at Christmas 1937, and married a year later at Christmas 1938; we parted just after Christmas 1939, at 22. Three idyllic years of love and happiness. Now we had seen each other, counting leaves, six weeks out of five years and eight months, and the last four years and seven months not at all, so what could one expect? To be apart for almost twice as long as we had previously known one another…

It is hard to remember those first 2 or 3 weeks. I don't think we made a big thing about it, but it was very chancy. Fortunately, my mother was a tower of strength in her support for both of us. She had come to love Mary as her own daughter, and I have no doubt she persuaded us to give each other a chance.

Mary and I decided, towards the end of my leave, to spend a week's holiday up in London. We went up by train. On spec, Mary suggested calling on her cousin, who had a taxi business in central London. He warned us that his digs could be hard to find, but he was kindness itself, and he found a very nice lady who let rooms. We had a splendid room with a huge bay window, and bed and breakfast. We dined out every day and visited a lot of shows etc. At the end of the week we began to realise that we still had a spark on which to build again. We were now 28 years and a few months each.

Returning from leave I was sent to Southowram, which was a nissen hut camp overlooking Halifax. There was a regimental Sergeant Major who had a military medal up, and he noticed that I was a Staff Sergeant with the Oak Leaf for mentioned in despatches, the Africa Star with the 8th Army Bar, the Italian star etc. As there were several hundred men in camp every morning, a parade was called, and route march and various jobs had to be done. However, after the first morning parade, he came over to chat with me about war experiences, and he ended with telling me that I had no need to parade on any other things.

It was not bad, but boring, and after five weeks of waiting for a posting, it came through for me to report to the dock at Maresfield, down South, with full kit.

The train arrived at the nearest station, and I caught a bus. I was dropped off at some park gates where there were a few houses dotted around. I saw a big house all lit up, so I knocked on the door and an officer's batman opened up. I told him what I wanted and he fetched his officer, who was a decent fellow. He told me that there was a military DCRE in one of the houses, but his staff were all civilians, and also that they closed their office at 5.00pm every night, so I would not be able to report until morning. He also offered me a temporary bed for the night.

The next morning I reported to the DCRE. He obviously was not expecting or needed me, but he had one of his civilian garrison engineers take me down to Brighton, where I billeted myself at Preston Barracks. Again, I avoided all parades and became my own boss. I became a member of the WO's and Sergeants' mess.

A civilian garrison engineer was in charge of some hutted building as an extension for Royal Engineer records office, and did not know what to do with me; I was told to assist him, which I did. The first thing I did was to find a room for Mary, which I managed through a man who had Desborough connections. So Mary came down for a week or two.

I had a very happy and cushy time at Brighton until just before Christmas 1945. I was suddenly posted to Tilbury where a huge camp was being built by German prisoners of war. I had leave home for Christmas. Before I left, we had a raffle, and I won a number of surplus commodities. Among them was a huge bottle of camp coffee.

Starting back at Tilbury after leave, I soon found out that they really wanted someone like me some six months previously, and there was nothing for me to do together with two others. So we had to keep out of the way. I also found the 48 hours leave could be applied for certain weekends, so I applied for a pass putting down 72 hours, because being a little naïve as I had not soldiered in England for years I thought it would be 48 hours plus travel time; a lovely 48 hours leave.

When I got back three days later, my colleagues said "you are 24 hours AWOL, and the Major has been telephoning the billet for you to report to his office", so I reported. I explained that being new to England I has inadvertently applied for a 72 hour pass by mistake, but as he had signed it there was nothing we could do. He told me he was not bothered about me being late but RE records had sent him my beautiful illuminated certificate for Mention in Despatches from the war office to present to me in some style, which pleased him greatly. The only thing was that whilst at Brighton record office, a clerk saw the Oak Leaf up on my ribbons and asked me if I had ever received an illuminated certificate. I said no, and this was the result.

> By the KING'S Order the name of
> Staff-Sergeant D.A.Marlow,
> Royal Engineers,
> was published in the London Gazette on
> 24 August, 1944,
> as mentioned in a Despatch for distinguished service.
> I am charged to record
> His Majesty's high appreciation.
>
> Secretary of State for War

Shortly after, I left for home complete with my army pay-book stating that I had an exemplary record and recommending me strongly for any job I might apply for. So, on 6th February 1946, I went to Northampton to receive my discharge and civilian clothes.

APPENDIX A

I did not mention that whilst on leave in Desborough in November 1945, I was having a drink with my father in the Working Men's Club, when who should come through the door but my brother, Norman. We were overjoyed to see him, but were appalled at how emaciated he was, so later on other leaves we got together and designed a pair of houses. We started digging the foundations on my demob, 6th February 1946.

After his release from a Japanese Prisoner of War camp, Norman had been conveyed by a hospital ship from Mukden in Manchuria to Vancouver, thence by train to an eastern port in America, and then by ship to England. He was given remedial treatment during the whole journey, after having been starved for three and a half years. When he reached Desborough one night in November 1945 and met our father and I, he was a shadow of his former self.

Fortunately, having a basically strong constitution, he recovered quickly, and by February 6th, when I was demobbed with 16 weeks leave (a day for every month I had served abroad) and Norman had 4 months sick leave, we designed and built a pair of new houses, with some difficulties over materials, but completed and moved in on Norman's birthday, June 22nd 1946.

APPENDIX B - POEM

The following is a poem I sent to my mother, which she had published in the local newspaper.

Made in the USA
Lexington, KY
25 February 2013